Sundries Of A

Poetic Soul

A heartfelt sundry of poems

Janae Stewart

SUNDRIES

SUNDRIES OF A POETIC SOUL

Copyright © 2015 Janae Stewart

All rights reserved. No part of this book may be reproduced or transmitted in any form or by any means, electronic or mechanical, including photocopying, recording, or by any information storage and retrieval system, without permission in writing from the publisher. All questions and/or request are to be submitted to: 134 Andrew Drive, Reidsville NC, 27320.

To the best of said publisher knowledge, this is an original manuscript and is the sole property of author **JANAE STEWART**

Printed in the United States of America

ISBN-13:978-0692594506
ISBN-10:0692594507

Printed by Createspace 2015

Published by BlaqRayn Publishing Plus 2015

Sundries Of A

Poetic

Soul

A heartfelt sundry of poems

Janae Stewart

SUNDRIES

The Hair Root of History (Nove Otto)

The hair root of history,

Of motivational speakers who inspire me.

Looking through the roots of my hair length.

The roots of my labor all in my history that portrays me.

Finding through the leaders finding my strength,

Combing and brushing with leaders entwined.

Looking through the length of my hair of history lining.

SUNDRIES

Heaven's Name (Lento Poem)

Live by the word and what is said.

See eye to eye on heaven's earth.

Sky got our names in heaven in our own bed.

Existing by heaven's name back to child's birth.

Rude of have none or any.

Gates that opens for many.

Food of soul complementing plenty.

Waits for no more pain for all the attendees.

Father Can You Hear Me (Richter meter)

Prayer,

On hands and knees,

Begging the good Lord, Please.

Giving his love and strength to me.

He never leaves me always in my soul.

God you keep my strength in his soul.

I have you in my soul.

What would I do?

Prayer

SUNDRIES

Happy Couples (Octallel)

Happy couples with passion kiss.

Commemorating wedding bliss.

Sensual romantic kiss,

Brilliant sensation of this.

Intimacy with just me,

Showing together to be,

Happy couples with passion kiss,

Commemorating wedding bliss.

King and Queen (Irregular Ode)

A castle that unites,

Sitting in there royal throne.

King and queen delight,

A joker with laughter of his own,

The king and queen smiles ear to ear.

Passionate kisses of silent tone.

With different expression of joyous very near,

Everyone bowing to the king and queen in there zone.

King and queen full of life,

Smiling crowd as king and queen wave.

Hands of laughter,

As the king and queen sit on their throne.

A castle full of love all not their own,

Kings and queen of majesty,

Showing nothing but there casualty.

SUNDRIES

I Can't Stand You (Octave Poetry)

Boy, why do I bother being with you.

You always putting our relationship as a test.

Knowing, there is no way to fix this mess.

Seeing the crazy things you do.

Boy, I put my hands up to say bye.

Your life, my life can't stand each other intimately.

Why, do I even try?

SUNDRIES

Kisses (Trinet)

Kisses,

My lips,

And his lips,

Our love everlasting.

Puckered,

Kisses,

His Lips.

His Touch (Parallel de Crystalline)

Hold around

My waist, he does I smile.

Loving the way he place his smiles too.

 Hey there boo,

As I feel the touch on my skin.

It is him, I feel a glow within.

Our Love (The Blitz Poem)

Our love shows we are a couple.

In the he way we show each other.

Why are we still together?

Why because we have a child?

The bed we share is cold.

The way we share our love is gone.

At the end, no one really sees this side.

At the moment wondering what happen to our Mr. and Mrs.

There is no happiness.

We still do what we are supposed to do.

We continue to love without saying the words, I love you.

In bed, I lay on one side you lay on another.

In our home, we pretend we are something that we are not.

Trying to show on the outside that our love is hot.

Trying to portray a love that is not.

Tears (Joseph's Star)

Tears,

Water filled,

Try to hold back.

 Her pain all in a napkin.

No one knows her attention,

As she holds her head.

Holding cries of,

Tears are

Dry.

SUNDRIES

Dancing (Kyrielle Sonnet)

One, two, step would you like to learn.

Up, up, down, down and turn.

Hand flex palm and hand stretch let's see what's next.

Take your left leg up and flex.

Plié a little stretch your root foot with a point.

Stand up straight and stretch your joint.

Yes, not a cardiac workout, but you will feel the context.

Take your left leg up and flex.

Now put your leg straight out in the air.

Your almost there.

As the crowd applaud, as they see your dancing becoming complex.

Take your left leg up and flex.

One, two, step would you like to learn.

Take your left leg up and flex.

SUNDRIES

Chapter Love (Triolet)

A love written into a book.

Holding words into each other's hand.

Always a chapter of ingredients unto looking at a cookbook.

A love written into a book.

Contents of relationship taking another look.

Chapter of words showing each other you understand.

A love written into a book.

Holding words into each other hand.

SUNDRIES

Painted Chain (Nonet)

He painted his chains to get away.

The consistency he portray.

The chain ultimate defeat.

Color chain takes a seat.

Asking the word why?

Soul knows the lie.

Painted chains,

Unlocked,

Not.

SUNDRIES

Her Brown Eyes (Clerihew)

She hides her eyes from the sun.

As her brown hazel eyes shows, she is the natural one.

Her natural nature is what is seen.

As the sunshine of the sun showing her eyes as a hazelnut dream.

Masked (Nanni)

Disguising masked who,

Definition of me,

Trying to find her way,

No one else could see.

SUNDRIES

Bride (Ethree)

I'm

His bride.

He shows his

 Happiness by

The way he treats me. He laughs, he smiles, sitting

Next to me I feel lovely.

My husband got me here laughing,

It is nothing but good smiling fun.

My husband and me. We are number one.

Warrior (Septolet)

Warrior,

Nile Queen.

Throne bond dream,

Passionate delight.

Highest,

River flows,

Bowing to her.

SUNDRIES

Schooling (Tyburn)

Looking,

Booking,

Cooking,

Hooking,

Looking, booking into the lesson. Hooking, cooking comes with stressing.

SUNDRIES

Acrylic Nails (Petrarchan)

His chocolate chest those nails are all over him.

Painting acrylic nails resisting as it's a dream.

These acrylic nails going everywhere, there are very extreme.

Nails came all out like a beam.

Singing with a chocolate chest as it a solo hymn.

He feels them of sudden exposure.

As he feels the touch of acrylic nails on his skin.

His chest feels the way of the acrylic nails begin.

Loving this chocolate man of mahogany.

The acrylic nails of him being bodily.

SUNDRIES

Another Girl

When she looks in the mirror what does she see.

She doesn't see her.

She sees another girl.

Her smile gone.

Her face of making everyone laugh.

What happened to her?

She sees another girl.

No one will understand her world.

Her scars are deceit.

She looks back at herself.

She feels she needs to look back at herself again and again.

Is what her defeat is.

She got to look back at herself.

She needs to say" Yes, I see another girl."

I am beautiful in my own world.

SUNDRIES

The Skin I'm In (Fibonacci)

I want

To be

The woman

That everyone loves.

Her colors is mahogany.

She is a strong black woman not because of her content.

Judge her the way she carries herself. She proves to be her ultimate being.

How she shows her physically characteristics mentally and physically. Showing you her heart and soul this is the skin she in.

Mommy Don't Want to Make You Sad (Rondeau) (Collaboration with Zyaire and me)

Mommy don't want to make you sad,

 I know I was bad.

 Son if you know how I feel,

Just accept your consequences that is the deal.

 Look, Mommy I love when you are glad.

 See all the fun we had, I don't want to make Mommy sad.

Son, keep your mouth sealed. Mommy, don't want to make you sad.

Son, I feel like we are turning our talking into an ad.

Mommy, I want to show you and be your grad.

 I love when we sit together at the dinner table with a good meal.

 Son, are love for each other is concealed.

 Mommy, I hope after I make this letter for you I hope you're glad.

Mommy, I don't want to make you sad.

SUNDRIES

My King (Pantoum)

My King wears a crown,

As he sits on his throne.

Letting his queen do her thing,

Making sure his castle is safe.

As he sits on his throne,

King smiling with big embrace.

Making sure his castle is safe,

A queen is happy at her home.

As he sits on his throne,

Letting his queen do her thing.

A queen happy at her home,

My King wears his crown.

SUNDRIES

Superwoman

(based on Karyn White song) (my version)

As soon as we get up in the morning,

I iron our clothes for work.

Make our bed,

Make sure your stomach is full.

Got your cup of coffee waiting,

I see you anticipating.

I can't tell what,

I sit here and make your bath.

I remember how we use to sit in there together and giggle and laugh,

You don't want to do that anymore.

You use to give me kisses when you were going out the door,

What happened to us?

Now most of our time is us fighting and fussing, I try to be this person you want me to be.

I'm not Wonder woman, riding an invisible plane,

Or trying to train.

I'm not trying to fly to find out what is wrong with you,

- 25 -

I'm not a Superwoman.

I love you,

The way you're acting I can tell that you are through.

SUNDRIES

Child's Cry (Mirror Image) (Acrostic)

Child under despair
Hearing of cry
Impression of rising
Living without shelter
Despair of child

Child of crying
Raining of tears
Youth of no soul

Mentioning of
Eyes Wiping
No soul of youth
Tears of mining

Crying of child
Child of despising
Shelter without living
Rising of impression

SUNDRIES

Cry of hearing

Despair under child

SUNDRIES

I Opened My Heart to You (French)

J'ai ouvert mon cœur pour vous,

 Peu importe ce que nous traversons.

 Bébé, je t'aime,

Je vois que nous avons nous-mêmes fait-nous,

Que je suis assis ici et avouer mon amour.

On ne sait jamais comment nos cœurs devinrent forts,

Un amour ressuscité qui nous a fait aller longtemps.

Je l'avoue,

J'ai pensé que vous étiez un homme juste essayé de passer sous ma robe.

J'ai eu tort, les mots je t'aime poursuivre sa croissance très forte.

Mon cœur bat dans ma main,

Je suis heureux que tu sois mon homme.

Vous êtes céleste envoyé,

Coup d'œil dans quelle mesure vous allaient et venaient.

SUNDRIES

I Opened Up My Heart to You (English)

I opened up my heart to you,

No matter what we go through.

Baby, I love you, I see that we made ourselves we,

As I sit here and confess my love.

You never know how our hearts grew strong,

A risen love that made us go long.

I confess,

I thought you were a man just trying to get under my dress.

I was wrong,

The words I love you keep growing very strong.

As my heart beats in my hand,

I am glad you are my man.

You are heavenly sent,

Look how far you came and went.

SUNDRIES

As We Dance

As we dance,

We dance the night away,

As my soul entwine with your embrace,

You hold me at my waist.

As we dance holding each other,

Looking at each other face to face.

We dance the night away,

This is where my beating heart has got me for you embracing my soul.

A temptation unknown dancing, rhythmically under the darkness of the brightness of sky,

Just you and I.

As we dance,

Just you and me.

Made the two of us become we.

Fire (Mirror)

Red, yellow, orange together
Heating of flame
Desire of burning sensation
Heated temptation
Rising of the highest peak
Seeking of flames
Intensity fire
Burning heat
Hotness of soul Itching touch
Sensation burning
Heated Flame
Desire
Burning sensation
Touch itching
Soul of hotness
Heat burning
Fire intensity
Flames of seeking
Peak highest of rising

SUNDRIES

Flames of temptation heated

Sensation burning desire

Flame of heating

 Together orange, yellow and red

The Storm (Italian Sonnet)

The Storm sees our day and night,

Sometimes when our skies are blue or gray.

When it strikes thunder or light.

We get together no matter what our life is we pray.

 As the storm sees passes our sunshine,

The light is part of our completion. We are on each other mind,

Sometimes the storm needs a press button of deletion.

What happens through the rain or storm?

How much more can we take.

 Our ups and downs keeps us warm,

We will get through the storm.

SUNDRIES

I'm Still in Love with You

I'm still in love with you,

No matter what we go through.

Try not to break any of my words,

How you treat me is very absurd.

I love you,

Yes, I do.

I am still in love with you,

One day I want your hand.

I want you to be more than my man,

You keep hurting me.

You think it is okay,

Will my love for you fade away?

I love you,

Yes, I do.

The way you treat me, I won't know what to do,

I am still in love with you.

SUNDRIES

My Son (Kyrielle)

>My son I love you very much,
>
>Our heart and soul keep in touch.
>
>You are the one I gave my Earth,
>
>Love you more and more since childbirth.

SUNDRIES

Bonnie and Clyde (Horation Ode Poem)

This is to my Clyde,

Always shoulder to shoulder together.

Baby you know what we do you know how we ride,

No one can split up apart never.

Even when separation of you and me,

We still together as one.

People will never understand,

No one will understand our journey.

I'm your Bonnie and together we have so much fun,

Clyde where is the clip to my gun wrist band

Season Change (Rondeau)

The change of seasons rearranged,

Weather change for no reason exchanged.

As jackets goes from on to off with sweat,

Temperature rises is what the sun get.

Seasons of four unchanged,

With names of season as shortchanged.

Extravagant seasons prearranged.

From racing deer to swatting net,

The Change.

Four seasons of being changed,

Seasons are rearranged.

Changes of weather with a threat,

Winter not gone yet.

Four seasons are ranged,

The Change.

SUNDRIES

My World (Petrarchan)

As my globe keeps a twirl,

World that can't resist.

No Earth can't nobody understand what coexist,

My heart is a swirl.

My soul is a diamond pearl,

This is my breath in the mist.

My earth going into a twist,

I am my own girl.

My world in different colors of the occasion.

As my world spreads across the border,

Keeping my Earth and world above water.

Looking at the summary of Earth equation.

Trying to keep up with the throne of Earth queen,

Finding my Earth and world unseen.

SUNDRIES

My Trip (Villanelle)

As I walk down the road I take this trip,

I walk into a straight or curve line.

A drink of water as I walk I take a sip,

Feeling the wetness of my lips.

As I look to see how far I came from behind.

As I walk down the road I take this trip,

I keep walking like rolling of a video clip.

Trying to find the road I want to decline,

A drink of water as I take a sip.

As I walk feel the trees gives a nip,

Watching the road go past as I keep reading stop signs.

As I walk down the road I take a trip,

I just need to know if I should walk or what road to find.

I have to walk and be on my internal grind,

No matter if my sweat will drip.

A drink of water as I walk I take a sip,

This straight comes into a line of mine.

As I walk down the road I take this trip,

SUNDRIES

Love (Memoriam Stanza)

>As I hold my love in my two hands,
>
>Smile with a bright smile on my face .
>
>Love that can never be replaced,
>
>My boy that I love becomes a grown man.
>
>A drink of water as I walk I take a sip.

SUNDRIES

Baltimore Riots (Fibonacci)

Stop,

Look,

What we

Created

Once again with our

Race another disgrace. Why now ?

With our youth emotional because this is truth when,

Will we learn to look ahead another black man dead, because we try not to be who we,

Are a unit but want to unite the way we are doing this just is not right. I believe in get up stand up for what we believe.

So let us find other ways so we can save our city today. When is stop the violence going to come to proof now violence is more with our youth this is a shame. Another city will represent a bad name.

SUNDRIES

Natural Her (Tanka)

Natural Curly,

Smiles of beauty exposed.

She stares with glare,

Smiles all beneath her white teeth,

Her surface is strong beneath.

The Limelight (Limerick)

>The Limelight of horizon,
>
>Temptation of Verizon.
>
>Loving who she is through the night,
>
>The emotion in the light,
>
>Intimacy Admission

SUNDRIES

As I Journey into another World (ABC's)

As I journey myself into another world.

Be holding my emotion into these boys and girls.

Can't understand what time is this,

Dedicating for generational emotional bliss.

Every time I hear these words and what they say,

Failure of our new generation comes in display.

Generational uproar no positive role models knocking,

Hidden emotion of parents always blocking.

Intimidated by the next peer,

Joining gangs they think are dear.

Kindness of hugging needs to come with other,

Loving to our younger generation of sisters and brothers.

May we stop the violence and corruption?

Needling the children's abruption.

Outscoring because of what is on their feet,

Parents we need to stand up instead of taking a seat.

Quantity over quality over family taken,

Reaction is one thing that they see,

Stand up and handle the situation completely.

SUNDRIES

Time to make a turn for the worst,

Understanding devotional dedication needed to be rehearsed.

Values lost in souls of their own,

Watching and listening to their profane tone.

Xeroxing each other style,

Youth's mentality of thinking their fully grown,

Zest of our generation holding together on their own.

SUNDRIES

Worship Him (Quatrain)

    I worship him with my praise,

    My hands above my head held high.

    More than worshiping him on Sundays,

    I praise him through the devotional sky.

Love (Tetractys)

                              Child
                           Love of
                   Honest and Trust
            Loving is value specialty

SUNDRIES

King and Queen (Irregular Ode)

A castle that unites,

Sitting in there royal throne.

King and queen delight,

A joker with laughter of his own,

The king and queen smiles ear to ear.

Passionate kisses of silent tone.

With different expression of joyous very near,

Everyone bowing to the king and queen in there zone.

King and queen full of life,

Smiling crowd as king and queen wave.

Hands of laughter,

As the king and queen sit on their throne.

A castle full of love all not their own,

Kings and queen of majesty,

Showing nothing but there casualty.

SUNDRIES

The Dancer (Quatrain)

    The dancer graces the stage of display,
    Graceful dancer portray.
    Dances as music how her body sway,
    Music stops as dancer leaps away.

SUNDRIES

Music (Diamante)

Music

Repetition rhythmically

Calm freely

Vibration emotion happiness joy

Quiet independent

Sound harmonious

Dance

SUNDRIES

I Can't Stand You (Octave Poetry)

    Boy, why do I bother being with you.

    You always putting our relationship as a test.

    Knowing, there is no way to fix this mess.

    Seeing the crazy things you do.

    Boy, I put my hands up to say bye.

    Your life, my life can't stand each other intimately.

    Why, do I even try?

SUNDRIES

Standing (Alliteration)

Sitting doesn't solve anything,

Standing solves more.

A humble appreciation standing salute more than before,

Standing sign of peace.

Youth appreciate no sorrow understanding.

I think about my student studying that I was taught.

Looking up in the real world silhouette shadow of what was brought,

Standing securely with my patience is what I hand up too.

Showing silence and peace this is what these streets need,

Standing stomping holding up signs,

Showing stop posters and stand in our own line.

SUNDRIES

I Love You. (Collaboration by Zyaire and Janae)

I love you with all my heart.

I love you when the moon hits the stars.

I love you like the sun rise.

I love you when you open and close your eyes.

I love you so much it will never stop. I love you to our last drop.

I love you infinity because you give me your heart.

I love you when you give me that lovable kiss.

I love you in my heavens.

I love you as my heart is pumping.

I love you more and more as we walk that path.

I love you more than anything on the Earth.

I love you more than infinity of sevens.

I love you more than fraction in a math book.

I love you more than a hot soothing bath.

I love you.

I will always be at your side.

I love you with all my pride.

I love you Mommy.

I love you son.

SUNDRIES

- 54 -

You are my love my only one.

I love you.

SUNDRIES

Her Brown Eyes (Clerihew)

She hides her eyes from the sun.

As her brown hazel eyes shows, she is the natural one.

Her natural nature is what is seen.

As the sunshine of the sun showing her eyes as a hazelnut dream.

SUNDRIES

Masked (Nanni)

> Disguising masked who,
>
> Definition of me,
>
> Trying to find her way,
>
> No one else could see.

SUNDRIES

Faith (Septolet)

        Faith in me

        Striving

        Seeing hope

        Assurance Inside

        Mustard Seed

        Growth Enhancement

        Determined Faith

SUNDRIES

Heart (Cinquain)

Heart,

Tender eagerness,

Resolving determining feelings,

Showing each other,

Love.

Strong Black Woman (Acrostic)

Sometimes I just want to give up

Trying hard every day to be tough

Remembering every day of who I am

Observing myself not to fail

Never is not a word in my vocabulary

Growing of wisdom in my soul and mind

Bargaining with myself to do better

Launching myself to a better life

Advocating my soul into new horizons

Courage of legacy stands next to me

Kryptonite will not weaken but only strengthen me

Willingness and striving to show the power I have within

Outside and inside my soul shows lovable hearts

Motivating movement of my mind

Encouraging my inner thought more and more

Nature calling me as I live because

I am a Strong Black Woman

SUNDRIES

Don't You Hear Cry?

Don't you hear my cry?

I cry when you are far.

I cry when you are near.

I cry when I am sad.

I cry when I am mad.

Don't you hear my cry?

I try to hold my tears back.

It doesn't help very well.

I hold my cry in.

I cry when I am full of joy.

Don't you hear my cry?

Baby I cry for you.

You know what I do.

Don't you hear my cry?

I try to keep my composure.

I just want to know one more thing.

Can you hear my cry?

Don't you hear my cry?

SUNDRIES

Eternal Love

I birth you from the womb.

I held you there and protected you.

I held you until you came out.

My love was held for you for eternity.

I feel love for you like I feel like know other.

I cherish you.

You are my heart I cherish your love from the first start.

You are my only love.

I hold you.

I protect you.

You are my child I birth.

You're my warmest from the Earth.

You're my child from above.

Nothing but everlasting eternal love.

No matter what we go through.

I got nothing but eternal love for you.

SUNDRIES

Two Ladies I Love the Most R.I.P.

My grandmother aka Mom-Mom and Aunt Michele

Two ladies I love the most Mom-Mom and Aunt Michele.

 I can sit with them every day with tea and a piece of toast. They are both in the grave,

Two strong woman that were very brave.

 Let's start with Mom-Mom first,

When they saw her at the front door they would scream with a big burst.

 I love her so much.

 Even when something was wrong with her health,

Her wisdom was her wealth.

My inspiration has to be my grandmother, she made me the person I am today, I always look back in all wisdom that she had in her head,

 I remember when I was younger I didn't understand a thing she said. Now that I'm older everything she taught me is in my head.

 She was my grandmother I have the utmost respect,

In her wisdom she always made sure she had everyone on protect.

Her compassion for everyone you never felt alone,

SUNDRIES

She said she was always a phone call away all you had to do is pick up the phone,

She is not a phone call away anymore.

Her cooking, teaching, skills and words of wisdom always has my heart in store.

She was godly and so entwined,

She kept her children and neighborhood children in line. Aunt Michele was a type of another breed.

She stored wisdom into little seeds Aunt Michele when she got mad at you.

She would curse you out and ask if you are okay,

Then she will ask if you can bring a two liter Pepsi back her way.

These two people I enjoyed and love, Can't wait to see them I know they are in heaven up above.

SUNDRIES

Changing (Acrostic)

Could this be how the world is today?

Hollering and hounding on the words to say.

Accepting all the negative behaviors all around.

Not understanding the cry of help sound.

Going and going nonstop hearing nothing.

Intervention is not a click or anything.

Necessarily not understanding the outside.

Getting a pull of nothing to hide.

The Storm (Italian Sonnet)

The Storm sees our day and night, Sometimes when our skies are blue or gray.

When it strikes thunder or light.

We get together no matter what our life is we pray.

As the storm sees passes our sunshine,

The light is part of our completion.

We are on each other mind,

Sometimes the storm needs a press button of deletion.

What happens through the rain or storm?

How much more can we take.

Our ups and downs keeps us warm, we will get through the storm.

SUNDRIES

Raising a Son to be A Man (Mono Rhyme)

This is the plan.

Only a dad can raise a son to be a man.

A woman can try all she can.

A woman can teach her son to cook with a pot and pan.

A woman can teach her son to open the door for a woman.

A woman can teach her son to be loved by holding a woman's hand.

Even those were things that a woman teaches her son to be a man.

A woman can't raise her son better than a man.

In reality, this is what a dad and son supposed to learn together of becoming a man.

SUNDRIES

- 67 -

It doesn't matter who is raising a son to be a man.

It just needs to be a positive male role model that can

SUNDRIES

Snowflakes (Villanueva)

Snowflakes are falling lightly from the sky,

Wrapped gifts tied in bows.

In the winter, the leaves get covered in snow.

People got decoration with dye,

Loving the way it flows,

Snowflakes are falling lightly from the sky.

Sliding on the sleigh low and high, watching the snow from the windows, in the winter, the leaves get covered in snow.

Waiting for the snow to lye,

SUNDRIES

Medicine and tissues with nose blow,

In the winter, the leaves covered in snow.

Smelling and tasting pumpkin pie,

Feeling the comfort of blanket and pillows,
Snowflakes are falling lightly from the sky,

In the winter, the leaves get covered in the snow.

SUNDRIES

Marionette (Streamed Quinet)

Played with emotional strings,

Among other things,

In puppet stands,

String of hands,

Made my body sing.

SUNDRIES

Take (Florette)

I try to let the water take,

Expression of mental heart break,

Leave me alone there is the door.

Look I'm done,

I got leaves that need to be raked.

SUNDRIES

My Serenity (Epulaeryu)

Hearing ocean of music,

Dressed in white sitting,

My mind has nothing but ease.

Head laid on my knees,

Peacefully,

Sold.

SUNDRIES

Body Splash Box (Triolnnet)

A water box made of me,

Body goes in first.

As my body fills the lightness of the pool,

Splashing in the box is what you will see.

Natural chlorine is what the burst is,

My emotion in the water keeps me cool.

Head goes in first than after that my knee,

Splashing at the first beginning not being rehearsed,

3, 6, 9 feet pool is all the way to the top is full.

SUNDRIES

- 74 -

Loving the splashing all into a dimensional square box,

Swimming faster and faster running better than the jacks.

SUNDRIES

Conqueror (ZaniLa)

I'm a conqueror of being strong willed,

My King of my filled domain is what I proclaim,

A conqueror, a warrior is what I am,

I'm a conqueror, is what is in my name.

SUNDRIES

My Strength and Yours Together (Rondelet)

As we rock the strength of the world together,

We carry this burden and weight.

As we rock the strength of the world together.

We got the world of the Earth forever.

This world will never be our bait.

Our earth, our world will never become late.

As we rock the strength of the world together.

SUNDRIES

Hundred Dollar Bill (Rispetto)

My mouth is close with a hundred dollar bill,

I got a tear in my eye.

How long is this going to keep my mouth sealed?

Don't you hear my cry?

Yeah, right this makes me sad,

Hundred dollar bill supposed to make me glad.

Now you know food to eat, my mouth is dry,

A hundred dollar bill gone. Tears I'm going to cry.

Fire (Triquint)

My passion is forever on hire,

Heat existence of your fire.

Lady in fireballs,

As it falls,

Flame.

SUNDRIES

Africa Lady Mapped (RemyLa Rhyme)

Africa is the ultimate place,

Loving everything about it,

Having a festival full of food laughs and fun.

A lot of Africa country trace.

Map of Africa all arraigned,

African map seen all over the place.

The African music a traditional beat. Many countries Africa gained.

Lady mapped all of Africa,

Loves the dancing of her African feet,

SUNDRIES

Her way of greeting cultures are very unique.

Dressed up like a doll mannequin,

As wearing garments,

 Singing as she sways to get the water. Lady has huge bucket on her head,

With an African performance.

Sunset (The 7/5 Trochee)

Rise of everlasting sun,

Sunset to sunrise.

All in the lightness of the day,

Exploring of eyes.

Moonlight Wall (ConVerse)

Moonlight all over the wall,

Never let my ladder fall.

Taken me as the ladder stand,

Not leaving me without your hand.

Climbing to the night of the moonlight, until I reach the average height.

As the darkness helps me get to the moon,
As the bright skies hit the month of June.

Lightness goes into darkness of skies,
Moon sees me coming as it stays in my eyes.

The Strengthen Within Her (Terzanelle)

Her power has her filled,

A strength that no need can build,

Her power of her has her filled.

As green all over is sealed,

Nobody can tell about green envy,

A strength that no need can build.

Hulk is her explosion,

No one can see the green,

Nobody can tell about green envy.

SUNDRIES

Army of her as a Trojan,

Lightning bolts shout,

No one can see the green.

Feeling the thunder come out,

Her strength no one can see,

Lightning bolts shout.

Complacent as she could be,

Her strength no one can see.

Her power has her filled,

As green all over is sealed.

SUNDRIES

Why Are You Gone to Soon R.I.P. Aunt Rita Love You You'll Truly Be Missed

Why are you gone?

I ask myself every day.

You inspired me in so many ways.

You always had a smile on your face. "Don't get me turned up, "You use to say. Never thought this day will come.

You always had a story to tell.

I love all of them though.

Your heart and soul were pure of gold. I'm glad you're not suffering anymore.

I have a pain in my heart, I never had before.

I never ever wanted to see you that way. Aunt Rita, I love you.

SUNDRIES

I love you.

In my heart, and my soul you will always stay.

Those words don't get me turned up will never leave my side.

In reality, I am saying you're gone to soon my feelings I can never hide.

I know when I think of you there will always be a smile on my face.

I know you are in heaven's place.

Aunt Rita, I can hear heaven sing.

You are an angel fluttering with your halo above your head.

Floating above air with your angel wings.

SUNDRIES

Goal of Dream (Lannet)

I'm his ultimate goal of his desire,

The laughter of our love is on fire.

He has my smile,

I am all in his.

We are one plus one equaling us both.

No one will ever understand our fun,

His love and my heart beats more equally.

He knows I got him with forever,

SUNDRIES

He'll never ever forget how we smile.

I never thought I'll ever feel this way,

My heart beats like a drum, I want to play.

Showing we emotionally entwined, Capturing souls in a positive way.

He shows his love affectionate so do I, into goal desire, of each other's heart.

SUNDRIES

Diverse Universe (Minute Poetry)

At the world of the universe,

See it diverse.

Nothing but birth,

Of the round Earth.

Looking at the roundness axle,

What is Earth sale?

Tune into pearl,

Showing of world.

SUNDRIES

You Showed Me (Double Reverse Ethree)

You showed me how a woman should be loved.

You showed her it's in her mentally.

You showed her true love does exist. Never showed physically.

He keeps me on my toes,

Like no one knows.

My hands in the air,

He is my Earth,

Accepting,

Loving, Life,

Together, happiness is what we share. Our future together shows our love.

Our minds as bright as the moonlight. Husband and wife not even,

Our love can't be compared,

Sometimes fantasies,

Become real life,

Happiness,

You showed

Me.

SUNDRIES

Why Am I Still Trying (Terza Rima)

Why don't I ever stop it's not worth trying, my broken heart is an unbalanced scale weight.

I'm lost for words there is even no crying.

My emotion always behind a sealed gate. My eyes always rolled up high in the sky air.

Trying to be together is way too late.

My fist balled up real tight, nice and firmly fair.

Not playing with you no more, there is no love.

Why because no feelings, I don't even care.

Raising a Son to be A Man (Mono Rhyme)

This is the plan.

Only a dad can raise a son to be a man.

A woman can try all she can.

A woman can teach her son to cook with a pot and pan.

A woman can teach her son to open the door for a woman.

A woman can teach her son to be loved by holding a woman's hand.

Even those were things that a woman teaches her son to be a man.

A woman can't raise her son better than a man.

In reality, this is what a dad and son supposed to learn together of becoming a man.

SUNDRIES

- 94 -

It doesn't matter who is raising a son to be a man.

It just needs to be a positive male role model that can.

Family (Ballad Stanza)

It is husband, wife and baby.

Love that is shared with smiles.

A family of compassion.

No one can understand.

Whisper in Ear (A L 'Arora)

As I whisper in your ear.

Saying the words you want to hear.

I see you smiling.

As I'm laughing.

You smiling harder than ever.

I keep doing it more and more.

I can tell how I whisper in your ear. Feeling the gentle blows inside.

SUNDRIES

Grandmother's Cooking (Monchielle)

Love grandmother cooking,

Ingredients of love.

Her big pot on the stove,

Big Mama's her kitchen,

Where noses became drove.

Love grandmother's cooking,

Preparing food to eat.

Can't wait until my turn,

While serving the meal hot,

SUNDRIES

Smelling the southern burn.

Loving grandmother's cooking,

Pinch here of this and that,

Letting me taste the spoon,

Aroma so tasting,

Hoping it's done real soon.

No one but us can hear the whisper in your ear.

SUNDRIES

Romantic Lights (Gra Reformata)

The table lit with romantic candle lights. Petal placed from table to trail of bed. Darkness of lit night.

Loving the exposure.

My eyes open up to the romantic sight. As you kiss me on my forehead.

My feet up in the air on its own flight. Smiles from ear to ear.

Cloud nine is on the air.

Darkness made into a stars that are bright.

Followed feet of the petals tread.

SUNDRIES

Our love on our own height.

Smiling of eternity never stops.

Loving everything that is around.

Romantic lights felt just right.

Petal placed to where my legs have led. Leaving us at the end with having a pillow fight.

Loving this life.

Smiling more and more.

Jacuzzi nice and warm my body tight. This romantic nights giving me cherries fed.

Showing this little girl more happiness. The table with petal and candle light. Favorite food surrounded with designs of red.

Joyous and happiness no freight.

SUNDRIES

- 101 -

The most romantic feelings of the night. No one can tell the love that we have on sight.

SUNDRIES

The Morning Kiss (Tableau)

She deserves morning.

Kiss on her plush lips.

Every day same route.

To know she is loved.

Her heart fully pure.

Morning kiss deserved.

SUNDRIES

Her Tiara Doll (Aloutte)

Crown doll in her hand

Beauty queen she stands

Smiles no one else ever seen

Queen sitting on the throne

Tiara of own

Smiling in her dress of green

SUNDRIES

Musical Body Tone (Trinet)

Correctly played,

Hitting cord,

One cord,

Hitting the right cord piano keys,

A journey never taking a seat.

Playing keys,

Tone musically.

SUNDRIES

Sitting Next to the Windows (Harrisham Rhyme)

Sitting next to the window,

Trying to see all the sites.

Watching out for a television show,

Right out my window through daylight, looking at the way people walk all pigeon toed,

Occupying to make sure my time is right.

Paradise of Love (Patwah)

Paradise of love.

As wi kiss pon di temple of di castle.

fi wi hearts stands hearts beat across.

Temperature tone risen up to di highest peak.

Motion comes up to both fi wi love.

Mi love yuh.

Yuh love mi.

Fi wi paradise.

Paradise of love.

SUNDRIES

Paradise of Love (English)

Paradise of love.

As we kiss on the temple of the castle.

Our Hearts stands are hearts beat across.

Temperature tone risen up to the highest peak.

Motion comes up to both our love.

I love you.

You love me.

Our paradise.

Paradise of love.

My First Lady (Diatelle)

Mom

My first

lady who

I adore and

love. She would be my mom.

She brought me her baby up from

heaven. I will not ever be without

my first lady. My mother. She helped me through.
Mom

no matter what you know I adore you.

I will never be without my

mother. Love you dearly.

Mom, Yes, I do.

To my first

lady,

Mom.

About The Author

Janae Stewart, born and raised in the heart of Trenton, NJ, always had a passion for poetry. Drawing from her own life experiences as well as her knowledge on a variety of different topics, poetry had always come natural to her and from a young age, was the center of her life.

In March of 2006, Janae's first child, Zyaire, was born, becoming the new central focus of her world. Little did she know, Zyaire, at the age of eight years old, became her biggest fan and inspiration for diving back into the world of poetry.

With her son's support and her passion for writing rekindled, Janae began writing **"Sundries of a Poetic Soul"** in April of 2015, finishing in late August 2015.

Welcome to "Sundries of a Poetic Soul"

Janae and Zyaire Stewart

Zyaire is one of the youngest published poets and authors!

www.ingramcontent.com/pod-product-compliance
Lightning Source LLC
Chambersburg PA
CBHW031406040426
42444CB00005B/445